Cutie -
Happy Valentines
Day,
2020!

A Couple's Love Journal

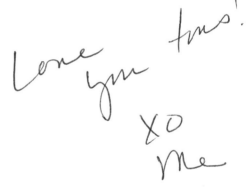

Love you tms!

XO
Me

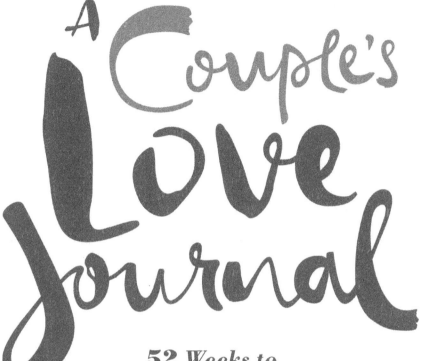

A Couple's Love Journal

52 Weeks to
Reignite Your Relationship,
Deepen Communication, and Strengthen Your Bond

LORI ANN DAVIS

ROCKRIDGE
PRESS

Interior and Cover Designer: Brian Sterling Lewis
Art Producer: Sue Bischofberger
Editor: Marisa A. Hines
Production Manager: Riley Hoffman
Production Editor: Kurt Shulenberger

Author photo courtesy of Donna Jernigan

ISBN: Print 978-1-64152-903-7

I dedicate this book to the readers. With a little effort, your relationship can continue to grow and deepen over time. May the discussions prompted by this journal lead you to a relationship that is better than you ever imagined.

Introduction

I truly believe that everyone deserves the relationship of their dreams—and can have it. I have a master's degree in clinical psychology with more than 30 years' experience in empowering individuals and couples to live richer, happier lives. Much of what I will share with you comes from what I learned from my family, my education, and my own personal experiences. I now live in Charlotte, North Carolina, where I balance a career as a certified relationship coach with homeschooling my two youngest daughters and working on my own relationship with my husband. I am committed to helping you create a relationship full of love and passion. My hope is that you will use this book to enhance your partnership, increase your communication, deepen your level of intimacy, and grow together as a couple.

No matter what stage of a relationship you are in, this journal will help you connect and understand each other on a deeper level through an open, honest, and inspiring journey you will take together over the next year. The journal provides you with 52 thought-provoking questions designed to inspire ideas and stimulate discussions that will celebrate and enhance your relationship.

In the beginning, relationships are exciting, but over time the newness wears off and meaningful conversation can decrease. Relationships can become routine and stagnant. You can have superficial conversations, instead of the kind that draw you closer and create profound connections. This shift can happen without you even realizing it. Most of us are not taught how to maintain loving relationships, and great relationships are more than just the absence of problems. They take intention, the right attitude, commitment, and effort, but the results are worth it! We all long for closeness and emotional connection with our partner. Relationships are a team effort and are created based on choices you make every day that allow you to grow and learn together, making each other a priority. Emotional intimacy is a key factor in the health of a relationship—it is a bond in which two people trust each other and feel secure and loved. Good communication is a major factor in creating and maintaining this intimacy.

Journaling as a couple gives you the opportunity to create a ritual of connection, providing you with new ways to share your thoughts, dreams, feelings, desires, fantasies, needs, and love for each other. You don't have to wonder what to talk about; this journal provides you with weekly discussion questions to develop your relationship, allowing you to express yourself in new and exciting ways. Journaling together helps you break out of your routine and expand your relationship. The questions are designed to help you learn more about yourself, your partner, and your relationship. These prompts encourage you to share at a more meaningful level, while also supporting your partner and building a stronger bond between the two of you.

I encourage you to set time aside to be present, give your partner your full attention, and be truthful in your answers. Make this an activity you look forward to each week—you can even add this to a regular date night. These questions could be great conversation at the restaurant instead of the usual talk about work and the kids, or maybe you have a favorite coffee shop or wine bar you could go to after dinner for your weekly discussion. Some couples may prefer having intimate conversations in the privacy of their own home. Set aside a specific time, maybe when you get home from your date night, to discuss your weekly questions. You could create a cozy mood for the two of you with candles and soft lighting in your bedroom, or you could talk over a weekend breakfast.

This journal is also a wonderful tool for couples in long-distance relationships. The options are limitless, so create something that works for you.

As an added bonus, the journal also provides you with ideas for ways to put the questions into action each week. You can have the relationship you always wanted, and this journal is the perfect tool to get you started.

LORI ANN DAVIS

How to Use This Journal

Now is the time to get started on your journey together. Let's talk about how to use this journal to learn more about each other while deepening your relationship. It is intended to be something you eagerly anticipate. Yes, journaling takes some time, but it is designed to be enjoyable time together. After some simple guidelines and tips to keep in mind, you will be ready to get started.

Keeping this journal in an accessible location where you can see it is important. Couples are often busy and you want to make sure you are working on your journal prompts every week. Start by agreeing to a set day and time when you will read the prompt together. You might be tempted to start discussing your answer to the question right away, but I encourage you to wait and give your answer some thought. This allows you to explore the topic at a deeper level before sharing with your partner. Take your time during the week to think about the question individually. When you are ready, write your answer in the journal.

You are provided with prompts to increase your communication, which is essential to the well-being of your relationship, but actions are equally important. Small gestures—a heartfelt smile or random act of kindness—can make all the difference. Couples can have a desire to do more to show their love but often are not sure *what* to do.

In addition to the weekly questions, you will also find tips related to the questions. These simple, fun ideas are designed to help you enhance your relationship through actions. You can use these tips in a variety of ways. Follow them as given or use them to spark your imagination and come up with your own ideas. You might want to keep a list of ideas to implement at other times. This can help you make your relationship a priority by doing something often to show your love. Your partner will feel loved and will want to return your love. It is a win for both of you.

You also want to choose a designated day and time to go over your journal questions. This should also be something you want to do each week. On the day you have set aside, show up and be fully present with the intention of connecting with your partner. Set the tone for the talk by turning off your devices and creating an inviting atmosphere. Take turns reading each other's responses. After reading the answers, feel free to ask questions. What do you want to know more about? Have fun with the discussion and see where it leads.

You can also use this time to talk about the weekly tip. Did you try it? What did you enjoy about the experience? Did this week's tip inspire other ideas that you might want to try? As you brainstorm ideas, be open-minded and creative—this can lead to engaging conversations about the desires, needs, and wants of you and your partner. When you are finished, consider a closing ritual—even something as simple as ending your time together with a hug and a kiss.

52 Questions

> *"Too often we underestimate the power of a touch, a smile, a kind word, a listening ear, an honest compliment, or the smallest act of caring, all of which have the potential to turn a life around."*
>
> **—LEO BUSCAGLIA**

When we met, what did you first notice about me?

_____

_____

_____

_____

_____

_____

_____

_____

_____

_____

_____

_____

_____

_____

Giving and receiving compliments feels good. When giving your partner a compliment, make it specific to them. Give them at least three unique compliments this week.

> *"Twenty years from now, you will be more disappointed by the things that you didn't do than by the ones you did do. Explore. Dream. Discover."*
>
> **—H. JACKSON BROWN, JR.**

What is one thing you have always wanted to do but haven't shared with me yet?

_____

_____

_____

_____

_____

_____

_____

_____

_____

_____

_____

_____

One way to show love in a relationship is to encourage your partner's personal growth. What is something they are interested in that you can support? You could go to a cooking class or sign up for a trial gym membership together.

> *"I find the best way to love someone is not to change them, but instead, help them reveal the greatest version of themselves."*
>
> **—STEVE MARABOLI**

Which of your partner's accomplishments makes you the proudest?

_____

_____

_____

_____

_____

_____

_____

_____

_____

_____

_____

_____

_____

Text your partner sometime during the week and say,
"I just wanted you to know how much I appreciate you.
I especially love you when . . . " Finish the sentence with
something you admire about your partner. Be specific.

> *"We cannot really love anybody with whom we never laugh."*
>
> **—AGNES REPPLIER**

When was the last time we laughed together? What made us laugh?

_____

_____

_____

_____

_____

_____

_____

_____

_____

_____

_____

_____

Sharing a laugh keeps relationships from becoming
stale. Laughter bonds you together emotionally and
leads to increased attraction. This week, find a way
to laugh together. Buy tickets for a comedy show
or watch videos of new or favorite comedians on
YouTube for date night.

> *"Your hand touching mine. This is how galaxies collide."*
> —SANOBER KHAN

What is your favorite way to give and receive physical affection?

_____

_____

_____

_____

_____

_____

_____

_____

_____

_____

Physical touch is beneficial to health and happiness.
It is relaxing and reduces stress while releasing hormones that bond couples together. Physical affection
is also a nice distraction from the rest of the world and
the stress of everyday life. Hold hands, cuddle, put
your arms around each other, or give a lingering touch
as you pass your partner at home; any touch that you
both enjoy is beneficial.

> *"If I could reach up and hold a star for every time you've made me smile, the entire evening sky would be in the palm of my hand."*
>
> **—UNKNOWN**

How do I bring a smile to your face?

Relationships can get bogged down with the heaviness of day-to-day problems and activities. Sometimes to-do lists do not leave much room for fun. Taking a break and making fun and laughter a priority is not only okay, it is also essential for the welfare of your relationship. Share a movie night this week. Watch your favorite romantic movie, or give your partner the gift of watching their favorite comedy, even if you don't find it all that amusing. You might laugh just because they are enjoying it so much.

> *"Appreciation can make a day, even change a life. Your willingness to put it into words is all that's necessary."*
>
> —MARGARET COUSINS

What do you appreciate the most about me?

_____

_____

_____

_____

_____

_____

_____

_____

_____

Communication can be one of the most effective ways to create and keep a strong, healthy relationship. Pick a time when you can spend at least 10 uninterrupted minutes together. Set a timer for 5 minutes and just listen to your partner talk about anything that is on their mind and important to them. While you listen, make eye contact and use nonverbal encouragement and body language to show your interest. After the time is up, feel free to ask questions if you want to know more, or proceed to share your own thoughts for the next 5 minutes.

> *"A kiss is a lovely trick designed by nature to stop speech when words become superfluous."*
>
> **—INGRID BERGMAN**

What gets you in the mood for sex, and what can I do to help?

_____

_____

_____

_____

_____

_____

_____

_____

_____

_____

Couples who make passion a priority are more patient,
appreciative, and forgiving of each other. Demands
of life can take time and energy while intimacy takes
a back seat. Try adding more hugs and kisses to your
daily routine—and not only a peck on the check or a
quick hug. Make your connection meaningful and sexy.
Try some big bear hugs and lingering kisses in the
morning before separating and when you reunite at
the end of the day.

> *"Couples who laugh together last together."*
> —**DR. JOHN GOTTMAN**

Which of our inside jokes is your favorite?

_____

_____

_____

_____

_____

_____

_____

_____

_____

_____

Laughter lifts your spirits, reduces tension in couples, and brings you closer together. Laughter is contagious. Look for humor in funny memes or videos on social media, in situations you observe, or experiences you remember from the past. Share those with your partner in a midday text or over dinner. Keep the laughter alive in your relationship.

> *"I can't promise that in our relationship you won't face any problems, but I surely can promise that you won't face them alone!"*
>
> **—ROSE HATHWAY**

What is your favorite memory of us working together to solve a problem?

Schedule a weekly meeting to check in with each other to see how things are going. Catch up on finances, children, your relationship, sex, and any other pertinent topics. This is a great time to discuss a plan of action, if needed.

> *"A strong marriage requires loving your spouse even in those moments when they aren't being lovable; it means believing in them even when they struggle to believe in themselves."*
>
> **—DAVE WILLIS**

Can you remember a stressful time in your life when I was there to support you? How did I help, and is there a way I could be more helpful in the future?

_____

_____

_____

_____

_____

_____

_____

_____

_____

_____

_____

Feeling frustrated or discouraged by life sometimes is normal. You can help your partner stay positive and optimistic by sharing an inspirational quote, story, or picture with them. Send your partner something inspirational this week.

> *"I love you, not only for what you are but for what I am when I am with you."*
>
> —ROY CROFT

How have you changed
for the better since
we became a couple?

Make time to call or text your partner in the middle
of the day simply to say hello and that you have been
thinking about them. Then ask them how their day
is going.

> *"You know you are in love when you see the world in her eyes, and her eyes everywhere in the world."*
>
> **—DAVID LEVESQUE**

Where would you like to visit on vacation, or where is a place you would like to move to?

During date night this week, begin planning your next vacation. Cuddle up and explore locations online together. You could even "visit" the destinations together virtually via Google Earth. Enjoy the planning process together, which can be as much fun as the actual trip.

> *"Touch is far more essential than our other senses . . . . It's ten times stronger than verbal or emotional contact."*
>
> —SAUL SCHANBERG

What is the most sensitive part of your body? Where do you like to be touched the most?

_____

_____

_____

_____

_____

_____

_____

_____

_____

_____

_____

Kisses, hugs, and touch show affection and are comforting and fun. They develop your connection and keep you bonded as a couple. Give each other the gift of a massage this week. You don't have to give a professional massage. Offer a light touch, a shoulder rub, or a foot rub. The touching is more important than the technique. Touching and being touched feels good.

> *"This is going to sound crazy, but . . . from the moment I first set eyes on you I haven't been able to stop thinking about you."*
>
> —LEIGH FALLON

What is your favorite memory from our first date? Why did you want a second date?

_____

_____

_____

_____

_____

_____

_____

_____

_____

_____

_____

_____

Remembering a positive experience you shared elicits warm feelings and is a great way to increase emotional intimacy between partners. This week, re-create your favorite date or one that was special to both of you. Enjoy living the experience again.

> *"The better you know yourself, the better your relationship with the rest of the world."*
>
> **—TONI COLLETTE**

During the course of our relationship, have you discovered something new about yourself? How did this realization enhance our relationship?

_____

_____

_____

_____

_____

_____

_____

_____

_____

_____

_____

_____

We are always changing and growing, no matter what
our age! Find a new activity to suggest doing with
your partner this weekend, like kayaking or cooking an
exotic meal together.

> *"Retirement, a time to do what you want to do, when you want to do it, where you want to do it, and, how you want to do it."*
>
> —CATHERINE PULSIFER

Where would you like to live when we retire? What lifestyle do you envision for us?

_____

_____

_____

_____

_____

_____

_____

_____

_____

_____

Dreaming together gives you something to be excited about, improves communication, and adds spark to your relationship. Fantasizing also helps you connect and grow as a couple. Spend some time "shopping" for your retirement home, no matter how long you have before that stage of life. Look at homes online or even visit some model homes. Enjoy the dreaming process together.

> *"The meeting of two personalities is like the contact of two chemical substances: If there is any reaction, both are transformed."*
>
> **—CARL JUNG**

Have I ever said something that made you change your mind? What was it?

_____

_____

_____

_____

_____

_____

_____

_____

_____

_____

Being a supportive partner requires being open to listening and also willing to take action. Show you care by being open to new things. This could be a new way of thinking or trying new activities that are important to your partner. Schedule an outing to do something that they have been asking you to do for a while, like attending a sporting event or going to a restaurant they have been wanting to try. Enjoy the experience because you are together, even if it isn't your favorite activity.

> *"The principles of living greatly include the capacity to face trouble with courage, disappointment with cheerfulness, and trial with humility."*
> —THOMAS S. MONSON

What was the biggest blessing that came out of our most difficult time together?

These days, with cell phones and computers, we do not put our thoughts in writing very often. Take the time this week to write your partner a letter and leave it on their pillow or the front seat of their car. The letter can be about anything that communicates your love. Share what they add to your life, a positive memory, or what you love about them.

> *"We come to love not by finding a perfect person, but by learning to see an imperfect person perfectly."*
>
> —SAM KEEN

We all have quirky traits; which of mine is your favorite?

Put on music from your teenage years or your favorite new music, then dance, sing, and act silly like you did when you were kids. Let loose and enjoy. Dancing is good physical exercise, as well as a wonderful way to decrease your stress level and create memories together.

> *"Learning is a treasure that will follow its owner everywhere."*
>
> **—CHINESE PROVERB**

What is one thing you would like to learn about (or learn to do)?

One way to become a better partner is by supporting your partner's dreams. Be on the lookout for resources that support your partner's dreams or goals. Buy your partner a small gift that might encourage them to pursue their goals. For example, if they mention wanting to write a blog, give them a book about getting started.

> *"Passion lingers on a state of bliss;*
> *Love loves you more when you kiss."*
> —MUNIA KHAN

What do you wish I knew about our sex life?

Couples who have active sex lives talk more, communicate better, have more fun, and are happier in general with their relationship. Make sex a priority. Send a text during the day that says something like, "Meet me tonight, 9 p.m., our bedroom."

> *"I saw that you were perfect, and so I loved you. Then I saw that you were not perfect, and I loved you even more."*
>
> **—ANGELITA LIM**

What excited you the most about us becoming a couple?

A great way to make memories is by reliving old ones. During dinner this week, reminisce about your favorite dating memories.

> *"When we love, we always strive to become better than we are. When we strive to become better than we are, everything around us becomes better too."*
>
> **—PAULO COELHO**

What do you consider to be your greatest strength?

_____

_____

_____

_____

_____

_____

_____

_____

_____

_____

_____

_____

Make a list of the things you respect, admire, and appreciate about your partner. Then share those either one at time throughout the week or put them in writing and leave the note as a surprise someplace where they will find it.

> *"You don't love someone because they're a dream of perfection. You love them because of the way they meet their challenges, how they struggle to overcome. You love them because together you bring out the best in each other."*
>
> —LANI WENDT YOUNG

During the beginning of our relationship, what was the biggest challenge that we had to overcome to be together?

_____

_____

_____

_____

_____

_____

_____

_____

_____

_____

_____

The number of positive interactions compared with negative ones in a relationship is an indicator of the health of the relationship. Sometimes we are unsure of how to let our partner know we love them. Make a list of how you feel most loved and share it with your partner. Help them know how to show you love in the ways you will best receive it.

> *"Grow old along with me! The best is yet to be. . ."*
>
> **—ROBERT BROWNING**

What is one thing you look forward to doing together as we grow older?

_____

_____

_____

_____

_____

_____

_____

_____

_____

_____

When you dream, discuss, and plan for the future together, you are recommitting to your partner and your relationship. You are sending the message that you are in it for the long term. Create a vision board together, symbolizing your dreams for the future. You can make a physical board, or do it on your computer and then use it as your screen saver.

> *"Pursuit and seduction are the essence of sexuality. It's part of the sizzle."*
>
> —CAMILLE PAGLIA

When and where do you most like to have sex? Are you happy with our routine, or would you like more variety?

_____

_____

_____

_____

_____

_____

_____

_____

_____

_____

Purchase a sexy game for the two of you to play or make up one of your own. The game can be simple. Try writing on pieces of paper something you enjoy that your partner can do for you, you enjoy doing for your partner, places you would like to have sex, and anything else you would like to add. Then, put all the pieces of paper in a bowl, mix them up, and take turns pulling one at a time.

> *"Physical connection is critical to emotional intimacy. When there's no physical intimacy, it isn't too long before the emotional intimacy goes, too."*
>
> —**KIMBERLY GRAHAM**

How satisfied are you with our love life, on a scale of 1 to 10, with 10 being the best it could be? What can we do to improvethat score?

Take time to set the mood for intimacy. Light candles, put on sexy music, shower or take a hot bath, put clean sheets on the bed, or give each other a massage. Take your time, relax, and enjoy the whole experience. Add more foreplay to your evening together. Spend time making out like you did when you were first dating.

> *"What counts in making a happy marriage is not so much how compatible you are, but how you deal with incompatibility."*
>
> —LEO TOLSTOY

If you could improve anything about our relationship, what would it be?

Let your partner know you appreciate all they do by offering to do something for them to make life easier. Surprise them by doing one of their chores without being asked or running an errand for them. Perform any small gesture that shows your appreciation.

> *"A good laugh is sunshine in the house."*
> —WILLIAM MAKEPEACE THACKERAY

What do you love most about my sense of humor?

_____

_____

_____

_____

_____

_____

_____

_____

_____

_____

Using humor puts things in perspective, lightens the mood, and helps with problem solving. Humor takes you away from the problem long enough to see things from a different perspective. Recall a time when things didn't go as planned and you used laughter to handle the situation and create levity. Maybe you remember a time you tried something new and failed—but were able to laugh at yourself and laugh together at the situation. Share this memory with your partner.

> *"She wasn't exactly sure when it happened. Or even when it started. All she knew for sure was that right here and now, she was falling hard and she could only pray that he was feeling the same way."*
>
> **—NICHOLAS SPARKS**

When did you first feel the chemistry between us? What caused the spark for you?

_____

_____

_____

_____

_____

_____

_____

_____

_____

_____

_____

_____

_____

The honeymoon stage of a relationship is full of "feel-good" hormones. Now is the time to bring back those feelings. Spend an evening holding hands, looking into each other's eyes, and kissing like you did when you were first dating.

> *"See there's this place in me where your fingerprints still rest, your kisses still linger, and your whispers softly echo. It's the place where a part of you will forever be part of me."*
>
> —GRETCHEN KEMP

How do you feel after sex? What is your favorite thing to do after sex?

_____

_____

_____

_____

_____

_____

_____

_____

_____

_____

_____

_____

Flirting is not only fun but essential to happiness in your relationship. Take time to whisper sweet nothings in your partner's ear or send a flirty text or email during the day. Flirting is a great way to build anticipation for what will come later. When you are in a relationship, flirting with each other can be a lot of fun because you can be more overt and risqué than when you were dating.

> *"Sharing the same passionate love with another person gives a feeling of being alive! The experience of something real is unforgettable."*
>
> —ELLEN J. BARRIER

What is your favorite way for me to let you know I am interested in sex? Is there a way you would prefer I initiate sex?

Do something sexy and unexpected this week. Cook dinner wearing nothing but an apron, run a bath and invite your partner to join you, book a night in a hotel (not for a vacation, but for a romantic evening), or take the day off work together, no clothes allowed.

> *"Alone we can do so little; together we can do so much."*
>
> **—HELEN KELLER**

What is one thing you would like to do together that we have not done?

Learn, explore, and try something new together. Keeping things new and exciting takes effort. Make a conscious effort to get out of your day-to-day routine. Take a dance lesson or a foreign language class. Expand your horizons together as a team.

> *"Let's not forget it's you and me vs. the problem . . . Not you vs. me."*
> **—STEVE MARABOLI**

How does it make you feel when we argue? What have we done successfully to avoid or resolve these arguments?

Relationships have ups and downs, good times and challenging times. If you want to be happy together, choosing patience and forgiveness is important. This week, be on the lookout for times you may not be as supportive as you could, times you are in a bad mood and don't respond in a nice way, and times you don't follow through with something you said you would do. When you are in the wrong, apologize—and accept your partner's apology when offered.

> *"Memories from childhood were the dreams that stayed with you after you woke."*
>
> **—JULIAN BARNES**

What is one meaningful memory from your childhood I haven't heard yet?

_____

_____

_____

_____

_____

_____

_____

_____

_____

_____

_____

_____

Get out old photos and enjoy remembering experiences from your childhood, favorite vacations you took together, your wedding, or when your children were young.

> *"Sex is more than an act of pleasure, it's the ability to be able to feel so close to a person, so connected, so comfortable that it's almost breathtaking to the point you feel you can't take it. And at this moment you're a part of them."*
> —THOM YORKE

Is there something sexual you would like to try that we haven't yet? Is there something you would like to do more often?

_____

_____

_____

_____

_____

_____

_____

_____

_____

_____

_____

_____

_____

It's time to play dress up and add some spice to your love life. Go shopping for something sexy for yourself or for your partner, dig out a naughty Halloween costume, or dress in an outfit you know your partner finds sensual. Have fun with this game. Spicing up your love life doesn't have to be serious. Being playful is okay.

> *"Always walk through life as if you have something new to learn, and you will."*
>
> **—VERNON HOWARD**

What is your biggest dream or goal you want to accomplish in your life?

_____

_____

_____

_____

_____

_____

_____

_____

_____

_____

Dreams begin in your heart and mind. Shared dreams
are more likely to come true. When you discuss your
dreams, you take them out of your head and bring
them into the real world where you can be held
accountable for moving forward and taking action.
Help your partner achieve their goals by discussing
them and giving encouragement. Check in on their
progress periodically in a supportive way.

> *"Behind every happy couple lies two people who have fought hard to overcome all obstacles and interferences to be that way. Why? Because it's what they wanted."*
>
> —KIM GEORGE

Can you think of a time when you felt we struggled to agree? Do you think we did a good job resolving the issue?

Set aside some time this week to reminisce about a time when you felt the most connected. Remember details about the event, as well as the feelings you shared. Savor the good times and strengthen your bond with each other.

> *"You will understand why when you look back, the answers are rarely given in the middle of the lesson."*
>
> —LEON BROWN

What is one life lesson you have learned from our relationship?

_____

_____

_____

_____

_____

_____

_____

_____

_____

_____

_____

Knowing that your partner notices how you are feeling—and shows you they are there to support and nurture you—feels good. You want to know you can count on them and they can count on you. Ask your partner things like, "What do you need from me today? What can I do to make you happy?"

> *"Sex is as important as eating or drinking and we ought to allow the one appetite to be satisfied with as little restraint or false modesty as the other."*
>
> **—MARQUIS DE SADE**

Do you have a sexual fantasy that you haven't shared with me? What is it?

Do something different for date night this week. Meet at a restaurant or bar and pretend you are on a first date. Dress to impress, wear your favorite cologne or perfume, pursue your partner, and allow them to catch you. Flirt and immerse yourself in your "first" date.

> *"We sat side by side in the morning light and looked out at the future together."*
>
> —BRIAN ANDRES

What do you envision our life together will be like in 10 years?

_____

_____

_____

_____

_____

_____

_____

_____

_____

_____

Planning for the future is good for couples. Looking ahead can alleviate day-to-day stress and bring a new level of communication to your relationship while focusing on a common goal. Create a bucket list for yourself and share it with your partner this week. Enjoy going over all the ideas you came up with. Which one will you do first?

> *"Love, like a river, will cut a new path whenever it meets an obstacle."*
>
> —CRYSTAL MIDDLEMAS

Is there a dream you had for our life together that is unfulfilled? What can we do to move toward that dream?

_____

_____

_____

_____

_____

_____

_____

_____

_____

_____

Good communication is essential for a relationship,
and texting can be a fun tool to use. Short, loving, and
flirty texts can enhance your relationship. Texting is a
fun way to add more flirtation to your conversations
and to show you are thinking of your partner. Send
them a text shortly after leaving home that says you're
counting down the hours until you see them again.

> *"Falling in love is easy. Falling in love with the same person repeatedly is extraordinary."*
> —CRYSTAL WOODS

What is one thing you are hesitant to ask me but really want to know?

_____

_____

_____

_____

_____

_____

_____

_____

_____

_____

A successful relationship is built on a foundation of
trust. Some topics are easier to talk about than others,
but being vulnerable and having the ability to discuss
any topic with your partner is important. One way
to open the lines of communication is by being open
and vulnerable yourself. This week, share something
personal with your partner. Let them know you trust
them to listen and support you. Then ask if they want
to share anything with you. Always keep confidential
what your partner shares with you.

> *"You will find as you look back upon your life that the moments when you have really lived are the moments when you have done things in a spirit of love."*
>
> **—HENRY DRUMMOND**

What do you most look forward to about growing old together?

_____

_____

_____

_____

_____

_____

_____

_____

_____

_____

_____

_____

Find a funny or sentimental meme or saying about growing old together and send it to your partner this week. Let them know you envision being happy together for as long as you live.

> *"You don't love someone for their looks, or their clothes, or for their fancy car, but because they sing a song only you can hear."*
>
> **—UNKNOWN**

What made you fall in love with me?

_____

_____

_____

_____

_____

_____

_____

_____

_____

_____

_____

_____

_____

_____

_____

_____

_____

Now is the time to remember all the reasons you fell in love in the first place. Then, share those reasons one at a time this week, maybe in a text or on sticky notes left around the house. Let your partner know how lucky you are to have met them.

> *"Problems should be like speed bumps. You slow down just to get over it, but you don't let it stop you from heading to your destination."*
>
> **—SONYA PARKER**

What is the biggest hurdle we have overcome together? How did we work together to overcome it?

_____

_____

_____

_____

_____

_____

_____

_____

_____

_____

_____

_____

Your relationship is a safe haven at the end of the day, the place you feel completely loved for who you are. This week, make time to let your partner know you love them just as they are, imperfections and all. Share with them how perfect they are in their own way. Give an example of some quirky habit they have that you love.

> *"The greatest happiness of life is the conviction that we are loved; loved for ourselves, or rather, loved in spite of ourselves."*
>
> **—VICTOR HUGO**

Do you feel I am here for you when you need me? What can I do better to show you my support?

Don't just tell your partner you love them; show them, today and every day. Make time to check in with your partner daily. Be emotionally and physically present when you are together. Give them the gift of your undivided attention.

> *"Setting goals is the first step in turning the invisible into the visible."*
>
> **—TONY ROBBINS**

What is your biggest career goal?

Ask questions about your partner's day, even if you don't understand much about what they do for a living. Listen to any struggles they are having, without giving advice. Ask about their goals at work, home, or school and what steps they are taking to achieve them. Ask how you can help. Could you give them some time alone on the weekend to study for a test or catch up on work? Be their cheerleader when they need one, encouraging them every step of the way.

> *"Love isn't something you feel. It is something you do."*
>
> —UNKNOWN

Was there a time when you did not feel our relationship was a priority? How can I do a better job of showing you how much I care?

_____

_____

_____

_____

_____

_____

_____

_____

_____

_____

Pet names or nicknames are a way of showing affection and tenderness. You might also have special words you use that only the two of you understand. This shows solidarity and intimacy. Couples generally start using pet names for each other in the honeymoon phase of the relationship. Continuing to use those names brings back the feelings of new love. Use your pet name or nickname for your partner in texts, emails, or private conversations to let them know you are still in love.

> *"When I look into your eyes, I know I have found the mirror of my soul."*
>
> **—UNKNOWN**

What is one thing about our relationship that you could not live without?

Remind your partner how truly amazing they are. Hearing this from your partner feels good. Be their cheerleader, to them and in front of others. Always speak highly of your partner around other people.

> *"Life is a journey, not a destination."*
>
> —UNKNOWN

What is one thing you would like to do that we can plan for the coming year?

Trying new things together increases relationship happiness. Pick something you have talked about doing together and make a plan that includes action steps and dates by which to accomplish them. Then start to implement your plan. Don't worry, you can make revisions as needed.

Acknowledgments

I want to thank Callisto Media for coming up with the idea for this journal and for allowing me the privilege of authoring this book.

I appreciate all my wonderful friends, colleagues, and clients who provided me with support and encouragement throughout this process. You are always there for me, cheering me on anytime I mention a new endeavor. Your support is invaluable.

To my family, thank you for being patient and encouraging me every step of the way. I truly love and appreciate you.

About the Author

Lori has a unique and passionate approach to love and relationships and believes that everyone deserves and can have the relationship of their dreams.

She has a master's degree in clinical psychology with more than 30 years' experience in empowering individuals and couples to live richer, happier lives. She provides relationship coaching to people around the world. Her practice spans the spectrum from dating for singles to working through divorce and renewing long-term marriages.

She is the author of *Unmasking Secrets to Unstoppable Relationships: How to Find, Keep, and Renew Love and Passion in Your Life, 365 Ways to Ignite Her Love*, and a contributing author of *Ready, Set, Date*. She is also one of the coaches on the *Radical Dating Show*.

Visit her website at: www.LoriAnnDavis.com

CPSIA information can be obtained
at www.ICGtesting.com
Printed in the USA
BVHW091936131219
566342BV00001B/1/P